INDIANA UNIVERSITY BASKETBALL TRIVIA

CARL R. McKEE

QUINLAN PRESS
Boston

Copyright © 1987 by
Carl R. McKee
All rights reserved,
including the right of reproduction
in whole or in part in any form.
Published by Quinlan Press
131 Beverly Street
Boston, MA 02114

Cover design by Lawrence Curcio
Cover photograph by Larry Crewell
Photographs on pages 158 through 180
courtesy of Larry Crewell

Library of Congress Catalog
Card Number 87-73290
ISBN 1-55770-027-3

Printed in the United States of America
November 1987

Dedicated to our lovely granddaughter, Elizabeth Marie Pallotta, who has enriched our lives since the day of her birth, February 8, 1986, the eighty-fifth anniversary of Indiana University's first basketball game.

Carl R. McKee lives in Terre Haute, Indiana, where he has practiced dentistry for the last twenty-eight years. A 1953 graduate of Indiana University, he has been a loyal Hoosier fan all his life.

ACKNOWLEDGEMENTS

I have attempted to make the questions in this book interesting, with some difficult and some easy but above all factual. Many thanks are owed and extended to Richard Roth, editor of the *Terre Haute Tribune-Star*, the Vigo County Public Library, Indiana University Archives, Indiana University Alumni Association and many friends who loaned publications for researching material for this book. My gratitude is extended to Larry Crewell, chief photographer for the *Bloomington Herald-Telephone*, for most of the photos in this book. The photographs of the I.U. Bloomington campus were taken by my son, Dr. Kraig McKee. A special thanks is given to my son-in-law, Andrew Pallotta, who encouraged me through this entire venture.

Last, but certainly not least, a very special thanks to the Indiana University basketball program, the players, coaches and staff from the past, present and future. Without them our Indiana winters would be reduced from the exciting competition they give us to a series of long, cold, snowy nights.

TABLE OF CONTENTS

In the Beginning
    Questions........................ 1
    Answers......................... 9

Hoosier Hash
    Questions........................ 15
    Answers......................... 21

Stats and Records
    Questions........................ 25
    Answers......................... 35

Coaches
    Questions........................ 43
    Answers......................... 53

Postseason Tournaments
    Questions........................ 59
    Answers......................... 75

Big Ten General Trivia
    Questions........................ 85
    Answers......................... 89

Holiday Tournaments
    Questions........................ 91
    Answers......................... 97

Players
    Questions........................ 101
    Answers......................... 121

Numbers and Hometowns
    Questions........................ 133
    Answers......................... 135

Photographs
    Questions........................ 139
    Answers......................... 181

In the Beginning

1. When was Indiana University's first basketball season?

2. Where did I.U. play home basketball games until 1916?

3. Can you name a year when the Hoosiers won the NCAA without winning or tying for the Big Ten championship?

4. Who coached the Hoosiers to national championships in 1940 and 1953?

5. Where did the 1940 and 1953 teams play?

6. When did I.U. move to the present Assembly Hall?

In the Beginning—Questions

7. Where did the Hoosiers play from 1960 to 1971?

8. How many Big Ten championships and co-championships has I.U. won?

9. Although I.U. has had twenty-four head coaches, only four have won Big Ten championships or co-championships. Can you name them?

10. How many postseason basketball tournaments has Coach Bob Knight won?

11. We know I.U. coaches McCracken and Knight won NCAA titles. Do you know a third I.U. coach who won a national title?

12. I.U. has a winning record against every Big Ten team but one. Which team is that?

13. What is that record?

14. Where did I.U. play its home games from 1916 to 1927?

15. Although I.U. has won five NCAA titles, they have only defeated four universities in the final games. Which university did they defeat twice?

16. In what years did they beat that team?

In the Beginning—Questions

17. Who was I.U.'s first All-American (he later coached I.U.)?

18. When did he coach I.U.?

19. Who coached the Hoosiers from the 1944 season through 1946, when Branch McCracken went into the service?

20. What third-team All-American, All-Big Ten selection and 1950 team captain later coached I.U.?

21. What years did he coach?

22. Who was the acting head coach of the Hoosiers for the 1970 season?

23. What coach won the first Conference Commissioner's Association tournament?

24. What was the CCA tournament?

25. Bob Knight is one of two people who have both played on and coached a national championship team. Who is the other?

26. Where and when were the championships for this other coach?

27. Although I.U. tied for the Big Ten championship in 1974, they played in the 1974

In the Beginning—Questions

Conference Commissioner's Association tournament. Why?

28. Although I.U. has five national championships, these have all been won at three sites. Where have they won twice?

29. What I.U. coach was known as the "Sheriff"?

30. Where did he play college basketball?

31. I.U. was a Big Ten co-champion in 1957. Why didn't they go to the national tournament?

32. Recent I.U. national championships and the 1979 NIT championship were celebrated around what campus fountain, as well as other places, by the students?

33. Where did the students collect to celebrate the 1953 national championship?

34. Who won the Big Ten in 1940?

35. Why didn't that team represent the Big Ten in the NCAA tournament that year?

36. What was the outcome of I.U.'s two games with Purdue in the 1940 season?

In the Beginning—Questions

37. When was the only time in Big Ten history that the last-place team, tied for ninth, moved to a first-place tie in one year?

38. Who did this team lose to in the NCAA tournament?

39. What was the extremely important I.U. game that was nearly postponed?

40. What was the reason for the near-postponement?

41. How long was the start of this game delayed?

42. Old Assembly Hall hosted the first Indiana State High School basketball tournament in which year?
    a) 1906
    b) 1911
    c) 1916
    d) 1921

43. This tournament was started by?
    a) The Indiana High School Athletic Association
    b) The Indiana Association of Basketball Coaches
    c) The Indiana University Boosters Club

44. What organization placed a four-foot-in-diameter, limestone basketball on the site

In the Beginning—Questions

of Old Assembly Hall to commemorate the winners of the first six state championships played there?
- a) The Indiana High School Athletic Association
- b) The Indiana University Booster's Club
- c) Sigma Delta Chi, the national journalism honorary fraternity

45. How many seasons has I.U. played basketball?

46. Who was the first I.U. coach to act in that capacity for more than two seasons?

47. How long had he been out of I.U. as a student before he was made head coach at I.U.?

48. Where was Branch McCracken from?

49. Where did Branch McCracken coach before taking over the head coaching job at I.U.?

50. Branch McCracken was named All-American in which year under which I.U. head coach?

51. What game climaxed Branch McCracken's coaching career before he came back to Indiana as coach?

In the Beginning—Questions

52. What I.U. coach, who was athletic director for many years, has an award named for him? It is bestowed each year by the "I" Men's Association on a living "I" man who has made outstanding contributions to the university.

53. Where did Everett Dean coach before becoming I.U.'s head coach?

54. What Dean and McCracken-era All-American later served as an assistant coach to McCracken and I.U.'s head baseball coach?

Answers

1. 1901

2. A smaller original Assembly Hall near the Indiana University Memorial Union

3. 1940—they were second.

4. Branch McCracken

5. I.U. Fieldhouse on Seventh Street

6. The fall of 1971

7. I.U. Fieldhouse on Seventeenth Street

8. Sixteen: nine championships and seven co-championships

In the Beginning—Answers

9. Everett Dean three, Branch McCracken four, Lou Watson one and Bob Knight eight

10. Five: three NCAA (1976, 1981 and 1987), one NIT (1979), and one CCA (1974)

11. Everett Dean at Stanford in 1942

12. Purdue

13. 60-90

14. The Men's Gymnasium

15. Kansas University

16. 1940 and 1953

17. Everett Dean (1921 Helm's Foundation)

18. 1925 through 1938

19. Harry C. Good

20. Lou Watson

21. 1966 through 1971 (he was out with illness for the 1970 season.)

22. Jerry Oliver

In the Beginning—Answers

23. Bob Knight (1974)

24. It was a postseason tournament sponsored by the conference commissioners for runners-up in the various conferences.

25. Dean Smith

26. As a player at Kansas University (1952) and as a coach at North Carolina (1982)

27. They lost a playoff game to co-champion Michigan, 75-67, at the University of Illinois.

28. Municipal Auditorium in Kansas City, Missouri, 1940 and 1953, and the Spectrum in Philadelphia, Pennsylvania, 1976 and 1981

29. Branch McCracken

30. Indiana University (1928 to 1930)

31. Michigan State and I.U. were tied with 10-4 records in the Big Ten, but Michigan State went on the strength of their 76-61 victory over I.U. at East Lansing.

32. Showalter Fountain

33. The Monroe County Courthouse on the square

In the Beginning—Answers

34. Purdue

35. The NIT, at that time, was a more prestigious tournament, and Purdue chose to go there.

36. Two Hoosier wins, 46-39 at home and 51-45 away. The *Indiana Daily Student* gives these wins as the reason I.U. was invited to the NCAA, even though Purdue was 10-2 in the conference and I.U. was 9-3. It makes more sense, however, that Purdue coach Piggy Lambert could have gone to the NCAA if he chose, but probably sent out signals he preferred the NIT.

37. I.U.'s 1966 season, 8-16 all games and 4-10 in the conference, to the 1967 season, 18-4 all games and 10-4 in the conference

38. Virginia Tech, 79-70

39. The 1981 NCAA final game against North Carolina

40. President Reagan was shot that day, March 30, 1981

41. Fifteen minutes

42. b

In the Beginning—Answers

43. c

44. c

45. Eighty-seven—it started February 8, 1901.

46. Everett Dean, for fourteen seasons

47. Three years

48. Monrovia, Indiana

49. Ball State University

50. 1930 under Everett Dean

51. A 1938 victory for his Ball State team over I.U. and his old mentor Everett Dean

52. Zora G. Clevenger

53. Carleton College in Minnesota

54. Ernie Andres, All-American in 1938 and 1939

Hoosier Hash

1. How are the Hoosiers announced at Assembly Hall?

2. What Hoosier native has coached the most NCAA champions?

3. What is the name of the floor that Indiana plays on?

4. Identify a popular slogan and poster during I.U.'s drive to the 1979 NIT championship?

5. What banners hang in Assembly Hall?

6. Why is the 1983 Big Ten championship banner there?

Hoosier Hash—Questions

7. What player developed such severe back problems early in the 1983 Michigan away game, I.U.'s fifth-to-last scheduled game, that he required surgery and was lost for the season?

8. At the end of the 1983 season, Indiana had to and did defeat three of the Big Ten's premier teams in a row at home to win the Big Ten outright. What teams were they?

9. What is the fan at Assembly Hall, main level, section F, row 46, seat 105 unable to see?

10. The five NCAA championship banners are displayed at which end of Assembly Hall, north or south?

11. What three flags are suspended from the ceiling in Assembly Hall?

12. Who is the present I.U. athletic director?

13. Who broadcasts I.U. ballgames on the I.U. radio network?

14. Who broadcasts I.U. ballgames on the I.U. television network?

15. Who sponsors the I.U. telecast with commercials entitled "Another Indiana Legend"?

Hoosier Hash—Questions

16. A Chicago commercial and operatic singer poses as a cleaning lady with a push broom singing "Indiana, Our Indiana," to open most basketball telecasts. What is her name?

17. Who is I.U.'s faculty representative to the NCAA and the Big Ten?

18. Who chairs Indiana's athletic committee?

19. How else, other than her name, is the commercial and operatic singer who opens the Hoosiers' telecasts referred to?

20. Identify the sports editor of the *Bloomington Herald-Telephone* who wrote, *Beyond the Brink with Indiana*, co-authored *Knight With the Hoosiers* with Rich Clarkson, and with Larry Crewell edited *The Champs '81*.

21. What is Coach Knight's nickname for this journalist, friend and I.U. basketball fan?

22. Name the *Washington Post* sportswriter who wrote a book about I.U.'s 1986 season.

23. What is the name of the book?

24. *Indiana University Basketball*, an excellent history of I.U. basketball from its inception

Hoosier Hash—Questions

through the 1975 season, was written by what I.U. Journalism School graduate?

25. The Indiana University Faculty Council voted "yes" to what proposal on January 20, 1987, that related to I.U.'s athletic programs?

26. What tongue-in-cheek method of retaliation did Coach Knight choose to harass the I.U. Faculty Council?

27. What were his suggestions for fans to recommend to the council?

28. Who was the I.U. athletic director in 1976 when I.U. won the NCAA tournament?

29. A banner referring to movie actress Bo Derek was seen hanging from the upper reaches of Assembly Hall during the Hoosiers' 1980 season-opening exhibition game with the Russians. Do you remember it?

30. This man was an I.U. basketball student manager in 1981. His father lettered in football (1953-1955) at I.U. and later was a mainstay at tackle for Vince Lombardi's great Green Bay Packers. Name him.

31. According to a recent poll by *Indianapolis Monthly*, a majority of I.U. fans would

Hoosier Hash—Questions

prefer to see Coach Knight in a sport coat rather than the red sweater. True or False?

32. What Tim Hosey and Bob Percival book details Coach Knight's collegiate coaching career from its start to the end of I.U.'s 1983 season?

33. Who does Coach Knight refer to as Indiana's "number-one fan"?

34. What restaurant chain in Bloomington ran a give-away promotion relating to the Hoosiers' defensive accomplishments during the 1975 season?

35. What were the terms of the give-away?

36. How many hamburger games did I.U. have that season?

37. The two restaurants gave away more than
    a) 3,000 hamburgers and 5,000 orders of fries
    b) 6,000 hamburgers and 10,000 orders of fries.
    c) 9,000 hamburgers and 15,000 orders of fries

38. Four times in the history of the Indiana High School Mr. Basketball Award, the award went to two individuals making co-Mr. Basketballs. Indiana University

Hoosier Hash—Questions

recruited five of these eight young men. Can you name them?

39. Who were the three co-Mr. Basketballs not recruited by Indiana?

Answers

1. "Ladies and Gentlemen—Your I*nnnn*diana H*oooo*siers"

2. John Wooden of Martinsville, Indiana, twenty miles north of Bloomington. He would have made an excellent addition to I.U. basketball, except that he was a Purdue All-American. He coached at South Bend Central High, Indiana State Teachers College (now Indiana State University), and won his ten NCAA championships at UCLA.

3. McCracken Memorial Court

4. *Now*
   Indiana
   Take it all the way

Hoosier Hash—Answers

5. Nine in all: five NCAA championship banners, the 1979 NIT championship banner, the 1973 NCAA finalist banner (one of the final four), the 1983 Big Ten championship banner, and the 1975 UPI number-one-team-in-the-country banner

6. Coach Knight displays this one because he feels the fans were very instrumental in the Hoosiers' winning.

7. Ted Kitchel

8. Purdue (64-41), Illinois (67-55) and Ohio State (81-60)

9. A scoreboard and a time clock

10. South

11. The United States, Indiana and Olympic flags

12. Ralph Floyd

13. Don Fisher and Max Skirvin

14. Chuck Marlowe and John Laskowski, with an occasional assist from Steve Green

15. Farm Bureau Insurance

16. Martha Webster

Hoosier Hash—Answers

17. Professor Hayden Murray

18. Dr. Marianne Mitchell

19. The Broom Lady

20. Bob Hammel

21. "Hamso"

22. John Feinstein

23. *A Season on the Brink*

24. Ray Marquette

25. They voted "yes" to a statement of student rights, designed, according to the council, to protect the university's athletes from being abused.

26. He suggested that I.U. fans write the council to help them solve their present dilemma of deciding whether to recommend the planting of petunias or daffodils in an area behind the old library.

27. He felt red and white roses should be planted there since these are the school colors and roses are very American.

28. Paul Dietzel

Hoosier Hash—Answers

29. It said, "Bo may be a 10, but Isiah's an 11."

30. Steve Skoronski, son of Bob Skoronski

31. False—75 percent say they prefer the sweater.

32. *Bobby Knight: Countdown To Perfection*

33. Former Indiana Governor Otis Bowen

34. The two Bloomington MacDonald's stores

35. Fans attending home games could turn in their ticket stubs for a free Coke if the opponent was held under 70 points, free fries if they were held under 60, and free hamburgers and fries if the opponent scored less than 50.

36. Two: Iowa (102-49) and Michigan (74-48)

37. b

38. Dick and Tom Van Arsdale, Indianapolis Manual (1961); Delray Brooks, Michigan City Rogers (1984); and Lyndon Jones and Jay Edwards, Marion (1987).

39. Steve Collier, Southwestern Hanover; Roy Taylor, Anderson (1974); and Troy Lewis, Marion (1984)

Stats and Records

1. One Big Ten team has won more Big Ten championships and co-championships than I.U. Which one?

2. What is that number of championships and co-championships?

3. What is the only conference team to beat I.U. three times in one season?

4. The total number of games I.U. has played is:
    a) 1,545
    b) 1,695
    c) 1,845

5. There are only two times in history that I.U. has beaten a Big Ten team three times

Stats and Records—Questions

in one season. What years and universities are they?

6. Indiana won the Big Ten outright in 1980 with an overtime victory over which team at home in the last game of the season?

7. What I.U. player sank two foul shots to tie this game in the closing seconds of regulation?

8. Who set a then-Indiana record for field goal percentage in a Big Ten game at Wisconsin in 1975? Until that game at least one media member had labeled him as a "Can't Shoot Complete Competitor."

9. Of the following players, which two have never had a field goal percentage of 1.000 for a single game when they made seven or more attempts?
    a) Tom Abernethy e) Chuck Franz
    b) Steve Alford   f) Mike Giomi
    c) Uwe Blab   g) Scott May
    d Rick Calloway   h) Stew Robinson

10. Indiana came from behind in the last game of the 1974 season at home to beat which Big Ten team, 80-79, giving them a share of the conference championship?

11. Which player made two free throws to win this game with eight seconds to go?

Stats and Records—Questions

12. True or False: In 1960, when Ohio State went on to win the NCAA championship, they lost to I.U. at Bloomington in I.U.'s next-to-last game.

13. How many games did I.U. lose at home in 1987?
    a) 0
    b) 1
    c) 2
    d) 3

14. What was I.U.'s Big Ten record in 1987?

15. Which Big Ten teams beat I.U. in 1987?

16. Did I.U. lose to any non-conference team in 1987?

17. What was unique about I.U.'s away game in the 1987 season against Iowa?

18. Has Indiana ever lost a game at Market Square Arena?

19. Can you recall the first and only triple overtime game in I.U. history?

20. Of the 21 overtime games in the Bob Knight era, Indiana has won how many?
    a) 11   c) 16
    b) 13   d) 18

Stats and Records—Questions

21. Indiana has won _____ overtime games in a row.
    a) 8
    b) 6
    c) 4
    d) 2

22. Mackey Arena opened in 1967. When did I.U. first win there?

23. Indiana's first win at Mackey brought sadness because of what?

24. Which Big Ten game did I.U. lose in 1953?

25. Did I.U. lose at home in 1953?

26. After defeating Valparaiso in a home opener, 95-56, in the 1953 season, I.U. lost their next two games on the road by a total of three points. Who were these loses to?

27. Do you remember the four years in a row when I.U. was Big Ten champion or co-champion?

28. Which team did Indiana beat at home in the final game of the 1973 season to win the Big Ten outright?

29. Which Big Ten team, rated third in the nation, lost at Northwestern the last game

Stats and Records—Questions

of the 1973 season to give Indiana the undisputed championship? Northwestern had only two Big Ten wins all year.

30. Which two consecutive years did UPI's Board of Coaches name I.U. College Basketball National Champions?

31. Which Big Ten team beat I.U. on the road, 83-52, the last game of the 1986 season? They won the Big Ten outright and left Indiana in second place!

32. Which Big Ten team, other than I.U., did Indiana fans cheer for on Saturday, March 7, 1987?

33. Does Indiana's four consecutive Big Ten championships or co-championships constitute a record?

34. Which school, of those playing as many as ten NCAA tournament games, has the best winning percentage?

35. Which team ranks second in this category?

36. When did this ranking change?

37. What is the I.U. Big Ten record for most consecutive wins (all games and not just conference)?

Stats and Records—Questions

38. When was it set?

39. Whose record did I.U. break in establishing this new record?

40. Which game of Indiana's broke the record?

41. I.U.'s team record for 1973-76 was?
    a) 108-12 for .900 percent
    b) 105-15 for .875 percent
    c) 102-18 for .850 percent

42. Who is the leading scorer in I.U. basketball history?

43. Where does this player rank in all time Big Ten scoring leaders?

44. Whose Indiana University record as leading scorer did Alford break?

45. Does Steve Alford have the record for career best field goal percentage?

46. Of the three seniors on the I.U. team in 1987, which had the best field goal percentage for his career?

47. Who holds the I.U. record for career rebounds, rebounds in a season and rebounds in one game?

Stats and Records—Questions

48. Who is Indiana's second leading career rebounder?

49. What makes Bellamy's career rebounding record all the more extraordinary?

50. How many games did Walt Bellamy, Kent Benson, Ray Tolbert and Don Schlundt each play in his career?

51. Who holds the I.U. career record for most field goals and field goals attempted?

52. Whose records did he break in setting both these records?

53. Who holds the I.U. record for most points in a game?

54. Who holds the single-game scoring record for Assembly Hall?

55. Whose record did he break?

56. Who holds the single-game assist record for I.U.?

57. Whose record did he break?

58. Who holds the I.U. record for career assists?

59. What I.U. ballplayer is second in career assists?

Stats and Records—Questions

60. Isiah Thomas's 356 assists put him third on the career list. Who moved past him with 385 into third place in 1987?

61. Who holds the I.U. record for points in a season?

62. Who is second in this category?

63. Is Steven Alford's career free-throw percentage over .900?

64. Whose career free throw record did he break?

65. Who holds the I.U. career records for both free throws made and free throws attempted?

66. Where does Steve Alford rank in these two categories?

67. Steve Alford shot over .900 from the line for two seasons. Can you name them?

68. Only one other I.U. player hit .900 for one season's free throw shooting. Can you name him?

69. Who holds I.U.'s record for free-throw percentage for one game?

70. Who holds the I.U. single-game record for field goal percentage?

Stats and Records—Questions

71. What is the highest number of points in a single season scored by an I.U. team?

72. What team is second in this category?

73. Have 1975 and 1976 been Indiana's only undefeated Big Ten Seasons?

74. What, from the standpoint of a won-lost percentage in the Big Ten, was I.U.'s third-best season?

75. Who holds the I.U. season record for blocked shots?

76. What is the I.U. record for most consecutive, regular-schedule Big Ten wins?

77. When was this set?

78. Who broke this string of Big Ten victories?

79. True or False: Indiana holds the one- two- three- four- and five-year Big Ten records for most wins.

80. How many Big Ten games did Indiana win from 1974 through 1978?
    a) 77
    b) 74
    c) 71
    d) 68

Stats and Records—Questions

81. From the start of the 1974 CCA tournament through I.U.'s first game of the 1977 season what was their record?

82. Did Don Schlundt live to see Steve Alford break his Indiana career scoring record?

83. Whose Indiana career scoring record did Schlundt break late in his sophomore year?

84. What is the record for I.U.'s biggest margin of victory in a game?

85. Which I.U. player on the 1987 team had the best field goal percentage?

86. What is I.U.'s record against Georgetown University?

Answers

1. Purdue

2. Seventeen: eight championships and nine co-championships

3. Michigan State, 1979

4. c

5. Michigan in the 1976 season, twice scheduled and in the final NCAA game; Ohio State in the 1975 season, twice scheduled and in the second round of the Rainbow Classic

6. They beat Ohio State, 76-73.

Stats and Records—Answers

7. Butch Carter, who also iced the win in overtime with two more

8. Quinn Buckner. He scored a career high 26 points on 13 of 14 shooting for .929 percentage. He also had eight rebounds, eight assists, and four steals.

9. b) Steve Alford and g) Scott May

10. Purdue

11. John Laskowski

12. True—the score was 99-83.

13. a

14. 15-3

15. Iowa, Purdue and Illinois

16. Yes, Vanderbilt away, 79-75

17. When I.U. lost to Iowa, 101-88, it was the most points ever scored against a Knight-coached I.U. team.

18. No, they are 18-0 there.

19. 1987 Wisconsin away—I.U. won, 86-85.

20. d

Stats and Records—Answers

21. a

22. 1975

23. Scott May broke his arm.

24. Minnesota away 65-63. It was their 17th conference game of the season.

25. No, they lost three away games.

26. Notre Dame, 71-70, and Kansas State, 82-80

27. 1973-1976

28. Purdue, 77-72

29. Minnesota

30. 1975 and 1976

31. Michigan

32. Michigan, in their last game of the season at home against Purdue. They beat the "Boilers" soundly to give I.U. a co-championship in the Big Ten.

33. No. The record is five by Ohio State 1960-1964.

34. I.U., .771 (37-11)

Stats and Records—Answers

35. UCLA, .767 (56-17)

36. With I.U.'s win over Syracuse in the final game of the 1987 NCAA tournament

37. Thirty-four

38. The last three games of the 1974 season, which was the CCA tourney, and first 31 games of the 1975 season

39. Ohio State's record of 32

40. Their first 1975 NCAA tourney game against the University of Texas at El Paso

41. a

42. Steve Alford with 2,438 (1984-1987)

43. Second behind Mike McGee of Michigan, who had 2,439

44. Don Schlundt's 2,192 (1952-1955)

45. No. He ranks seventh in this category with percentage of .533 (898 of 1685)

46. Daryl Thomas with a percentage of .541 (399 of 737)

47. Walt Bellamy: 1088 (1959-1961); 428 (1961 season); and 33 (Michigan in 1961)

Stats and Records—Answers

48. Kent Benson: 1031 (1974-1977)

49. He played only three years compared to the four played by some leading rebounders such as Kent Benson, Ray Tolbert and Don Schlundt.

50. Bellamy played 70, Tolbert 127, Benson 114 and Schlundt 94.

51. Steve Alford with 898 field goals and 1685 attempts

52. Mike Woodson's records of 821 field goals and 1626 attempts (1977-1980)

53. Jimmy Rayl, 56 against Michigan State in 1963 and against Minnesota in 1962 (OT)

54. Steve Alford, 42 against Michigan State in 1987

55. Steve Downing's 41 against Illinois in 1973

56. Keith Smart (15) in I.U.'s second-round 1987 NCAA win over Auburn

57. The old record (14) was held jointly by four players: Quinn Buckner, Bobby Wilkerson, Isiah Thomas and Stew Robinson.

58. Quinn Bucker with 542

Stats and Records—Answers

59. Randy Wittman with 432

60. Steve Alford

61. Scott May with 752 in 1976

62. Steve Alford with 749 in 1987

63. No, it is .898 (535 of 596)

64. John Ritter's .862 (257 of 298) from 1971 to 1973

65. Don Schlundt 826 and 1076 for four seasons from 1952 to 1955

66. Third in each

67. In his freshman year (1984) he was .913, and in his sophomore year he was .912.

68. Jon McGlocklin, 63 of 70 in the 1965 season

69. A great number of players have been perfect from the line on 10 attempts or more over the years, but the top performance belongs to Ted Kitchel, who was 18 of 18 against Illinois in 1981.

70. Several players have been perfect from the field with seven for seven performances, but Mike Giomi against Northwestern

Stats and Records—Answers

(1985) and Rick Calloway against Minnesota (1987) were both eight for eight.

71. 2,817 in 1975

72. The 1987 team, with 2,806

73. Yes

74. 1953, when they were 17-1 under Coach McCracken

75. Dean Garrett, 93 in 1987

76. Thirty-seven

77. Last scheduled game (against Purdue at home) in the 1974 season through the 1976 season

78. Purdue, in I.U.'s 1977 conference opener at Assembly Hall, 80-63

79. True

80. c

81. 67-1

82. No. He died October 10, 1985. Steve Alford broke his record at Wisconsin on February 16, 1987.

Stats and Records—Answers

83. Bill Garrett's 792 points (1948-1950)

84. Sixty-five—in 1972 I.U. beat Notre Dame at Assembly Hall, 94-29. It was the first year for Coach Knight at I.U. and Coach Phelps at N.D.

85. Steve Eyl: 35 of 54 (.648)

86. 1-1: I.U. lost to Georgetown, 60-54, on a neutral court in 1979 and beat them, 76-69, at home in 1980.

Coaches

1. Who is the only coach to win championships in the NCAA, NIT, Pan American Games and Olympic Games?

2. Where and how long did Coach Knight coach as head coach before coming to I.U.?

3. Where was Lou Watson's home town?

4. Bob Knight's home town is _____, _____.

5. Who is the winningest coach, all games considered, in Big Ten history?

6. Whose record did he break?

Coaches—Questions

7. What is Coach Knight's total won-lost record (including his six-year stint at the U.S. Military Academy)?

8. Coach Knight has missed one year in postseason tournament play since he has been at I.U. Which year?

9. What was his postseason tournament record during the six years at West Point?

10. Has Coach Knight ever endured a losing season?

11. What was Coach Knight's record against Adolph Rupp?

12. Which coach has the most Big Ten victories to his credit?

13. Who is second in this category?

14. Bob Knight is third in Big Ten wins. How many has he?

15. When Coach Knight was suspended for one game in the 1985 season, who took his place as acting head coach?

16. Against whom was that game played?

17. What was the outcome of that game?

Coaches—Questions

18. What game was highlighted by Coach Knight's first sustained use of a zone defense?

19. With this defense, what guard did he hope to keep from penetrating?

20. What two players from the 1984 North Carolina team played for Coach Knight on his Gold Medal 1984 Olympic team?

21. The team of what former Knight player and graduate assistant coach did Indiana play against in the 1987 NCAA tournament?

22. Has Coach Knight ever had a season with a losing Big Ten record?

23. One present I.U. assistant coach was the captain and leading scorer on Coach Knight's first I.U. team. Can you identify him?

24. Can you name I.U.'s three present assistant coaches?

25. One assistant coach from 1987 left to take a head coaching job. Can you identify him?

26. Where did he go?

27. Who was the youngest I.U. coach to win a national championship?

Coaches—Questions

28. What age was Coach Knight when he won his first national championship?

29. Where did these former Knight-era I.U. assistant coaches coach in the 1987 season?
    a) Bob Weltlich
    b) Tom Miller
    c) Jim Crews
    d) Dave Bliss

30. Did any of Coach Knight's teams ever pass up an NCAA bid for one from the NIT?

31. What Knight I.U. assistant coach grew up four years behind him in Orrville, Ohio, and played at Ohio State?

32. Can you recall the name of an I.U. Knight-era assistant coach who served as head coach at Cuyahoga Falls High School, where Coach Knight was his assistant his first year out of O.S.U.?

33. In the 1975 season Rainbow Classic in Hawaii (an eight-team holiday tournament) the only coach without a technical was _____.
    a) Bob Knight, I.U.
    b) Fred Taylor, O.S.U.
    c) Bruce O'Neil, Hawaii

Coaches—Questions

34. In the 1975 I.U. season, head coaches' technicals for the year were scored _____ and _____.
    a) Knight 20-opponents' coach 3
    b) Knight 14-opponents' coach 9
    c) Knight 8-opponents' coach 15
    d) Knight 3-opponents' coach 20

35. Coach Knight's first victory at O.S.U.'s St. John's Arena came in which season?

36. Prior to that win what was his record at St. John's Arena?

37. What was Coach Knight's record at Mackey Arena prior to I.U.'s win there in the 1975 season?

38. Name a high school coach who became an assistant coach at I.U. under Lew Watson after two of his star players from a state championship squad were recruited by I.U.

39. Who was the South Bend St. Joseph's High School coach who coached both John Laskowski and Tom Abernethy in high school and later became an I.U. assistant coach under Bob Knight?

40. How many times has Bob Knight been Big Ten Coach of the Year?
    a) 9   c) 5
    b) 7   d) 3

Coaches—Questions

41. What two years was Coach McCracken named National Coach of the Year (once by UP, and once by UP, AP and International News Service)?

42. What two years was Coach Knight named National Coach of the Year (once by UPI and AP and once by AP and *Basketball Weekly*)?

43. What is Coach Knight's middle name?

44. Which Indiana assistant basketball coach coached four Class A state championship teams at Lawrenceville High School in Illinois, including back-to-back undefeated teams in 1982 and 1983?

45. Coach Knight is under contract with I.U. through what year?
    a) 1989
    b) 1992
    c) 1994
    d) 1997

46. At the end of the 1986-1987 school year, Coach Knight was tendered what prestigious award by Sigma Delta Chi, the national journalism honorary?

47. How is the recipient of this award selected?

Coaches—Questions

48. A three-sport athlete, he lettered in basketball in 1951 and later was an assistant coach under Coach Watson. Who is he?

49. The three graduate assistant basketball coaches in I.U.'s program in 1987 included both a former I.U. player and the son of a very well-known U.S. collegiate coach. Can you name these two and, perhaps, even the third graduate assistant?

50. In which game did the "chair-throwing incident" take place?

51. Why was Coach Knight given a public reprimand and why did I.U. have $10,000 deducted from their $1,000,000 1987 tournament share by the NCAA?

52. Why was the technical called?

53. This coach shook hands with Coach Knight before the game was over, he said, "because when the game's over, they're going to carry me off." He was right; his Fordham team beat Knight's Army team, 65-60, that year, the 1971 season. A year later, when both had different coaching jobs, Knight, using subs freely, beat this coach severely on dedication day in Assembly Hall. Who is he?

54. In Indiana's 1976 perfect season, Coach Knight grabbed which I.U. player's jersey

Coaches—Questions

as he came out of a game after making a couple of rapid-fire mistakes?

55. In which game did this incident take place?

56. Who took Coach Watson's 1967 team out of the NCAA tournament?

57. What was the score of this game?

58. What 1956 All-American I.U. football end now serves as the Hoosier's team doctor?

59. In I.U. basketball history, the Hoosiers have had 32 different All-Americans selected first, second and third team by one group or another. Which I.U. coach coached the largest number of these?

60. One of those 32 All-Americans was selected as an honorary selection by the Basketball Writer's Association. Who is he?

61. Following are the Indiana University Basketball All-Americans, listed in alphabetical order. Place them with the head coach or head coaches (there may be more than one) who coached them at some point in their I.U. career:

Coaches—Questions

PLAYER		COACHES
1. Steve Alford	_	a) Everett Dean
2. Ernie Andres	_ _	b) Dana M. Evans
3. Walt Bellamy	_	c) Harry C. Good
4. Kent Benson	_	d) Bob Knight
5. Quinn Buckner	_	e) George Levias
6. Everett Dean	_ _ _	f) Branch McCracken
7. Archie Dees	_	g) Edward O. Stiehm
8. Steve Downing	_ _	h) Lou Watson
9. Bill Garrett	_	
10. Steve Green	_	
11. Ken Gunning	_	
12. Ralph Hamilton	_	
13. Marvin Huffman	_ _	
14. Vern Huffman	_	
15. Ted Kitchel	_	
16. Bob Leonard	_	
17. Scott May	_	
18. Bill Menke	_	
19. Branch McCracken	_	
20. George McGinnis	_	
21. Jimmy Rayl	_	
22. Don Schlundt	_	
23. Jim Strickland	_	
24. Isiah Thomas	_	
25. Landon Turner	_	
26. Dick Van Arsdale	_	
27. Tom Van Arsdale	_	
28. John Wallace	_ _	
29. Lou Watson	_	
30. Randy Wittman	_	
31. Mike Woodson	_	
32. Andy Zimmer	_	

Answers

1. That is easy! Coach Knight

2. United States Military Academy at West Point for six years

3. Jeffersonville, Indiana

4. Orrville, Ohio

5. Bob Knight, with 366

6. Branch McCracken (364) and Piggy Lambert (364)

7. 468-169, for a .735 percentage

8. 1977

Coaches—Answers

9. He made the NIT field four of the six years he served there as head coach—1966, 1968, 1969, 1970—missing only the 1967 and 1971 seasons.

10. Yes—only one when he was 11-13 in 1971 at the Military Academy.

11. 1-1—he beat Rupp's 1972 Kentucky team, 90-89, in two overtimes, in his first year at I.U., but he lost to the Baron with his Army team in the 1969 championship game of the Kentucky Invitational Tournament, 80-65.

12. Piggy Lambert of Purdue, with 213

13. Branch McCracken, with 210

14. 201

15. Jimmy Crews

16. Iowa (away)

17. I.U. lost, 70-50

18. Indiana's 67-62 win over Digger Phelps's Irish at Notre Dame early in the 1987 season

19. David Rivers

Coaches—Answers

20. Michael Jordan and Sam Perkins

21. Mike Krzyzewski—the Duke Blue Devils' coach

22. Yes—one in 1985 when his team was 7-11 in Big Ten play for a seventh place finish

23. Joby Wright

24. Kohn Smith, Ron Felling and Joby Wright

25. Royce Waltman

26. DePaul University

27. Branch McCracken, who was 32 in 1940

28. Thirty-five in 1976

29. a) Texas University
    b) Colorado University
    c) Evansville University
    d) S.M.U.

30. Yes—his 1968 Army team. The Academy felt the Cadets would miss too much classtime otherwise.

31. Bob Weltlich

32. Harold Andreas

Coaches—Answers

33. a

34. d—Knight's "T"s make history; other coaches' "T"s only make statistics.

35. 1975

36. 0-4—he lost there with I.U. three times from 1972 through 1974, and by two points in the 1967 season with Army, 61-59.

37. 0-3—he lost there with I.U. in the 1972 and 1973 seasons and in an overtime game with Army in the 1967 season, 79-69.

38. Jerry Oliver from Indianapolis Washington High School. The players were George McGinnis and Steve Downing.

39. Bob Donewald

40. c—1973, 1975, 1976, 1980 and 1981

41. 1940 and 1953

42. 1975 and 1976

43. Montgomery

44. Ron Felling

45. d

Coaches—Answers

46. The Brown Derby

47. By a student vote for the most popular professor on campus

48. Don Luft

49. Dan Dakich (former player), Murray Bartow (son of UAB coach Gene Bartow) and Julio Salazar

50. The 1985 Purdue home game

51. In protesting a technical to the NCAA tournament committee representation, he hit a telephone on the scorer's table.

52. He left the assigned coaching area.

53. Richard "Digger" Phelps

54. Jimmy Wisman

55. Michigan, at home

56. Virgina Tech

57. 79-70

58. Brad Bomba

59. Branch McCracken, with 15

Coaches—Answers

60. Landon Turner (1982)

61. The coaches of Indiana University Basketball All-Americans:
    1. d
    2. a & f
    3. f
    4. d
    5. d
    6. e, b, & g
    7. f
    8. h & d
    9. f
    10. d
    11. a
    12. f
    13. a & f
    14. a
    15. d
    16. f
    17. d
    18. f
    19. a
    20. h
    21. f
    22. f
    23. a
    24. d
    25. d
    26. f
    27. f
    28. c & f
    29. f
    30. d
    31. d
    32. f

Postseason Tournaments

1. What team took I.U. out of the 1973 national tournament in the semifinal game?

2. When, where and what was the outcome of the next meeting with this team?

3. What was the rationale some people used to argue that this game wasn't played on a neutral floor?

4. Who took the undefeated Hoosiers out of the national tournament in 1975? Where did they do it?

5. What late-season injury hurt the Hoosiers in 1975?

Postseason Tournaments—Questions

6. What was the score of the Kentucky-I.U. game in the 1975 regional?

7. What was the outcome and the score of an earlier, 1975-season Assembly Hall meeting of these two teams?

8. I.U. has been taken out of the NCAA tourney twice by two different teams. Who were they?

9. In what years did this happen?

10. In 1984 I.U. beat a team in the first game of the NCAA Eastern Regional at Atlanta, Georgia. Many people regarded this team as one of the best collegiate teams of all time. What team?

11. I.U. lost the final game of that regional to what team?

12. How many times has I.U. been to the final four in the NCAA tournament?

13. Can you think of a year when Indiana placed two players with the same last name on an NCAA final-four all-tournament team?

14. What two I.U. ballplayers made the final-four all-tournament NCAA team in 1987?

Postseason Tournaments—Questions

15. Who was the most valuable player on this all-tournament team?

16. An injury to what I.U. player, in the first half of the 1987 final game against Syracuse, hurt I.U.'s chances?

17. What three similarities are there between Rick Calloway's participation in the final NCAA game of 1987 and Bobby Wilkerson's participation in the final NCAA game of 1976?

18. Indiana won their final four games of the 1987 NCAA by a total of how many points?
    a) 10
    b) 12
    c) 14
    d) 16

19. What six teams did I.U. defeat and in what order to win the 1987 NCAA?

20. What team has I.U. beaten the most in NCAA tournament play?

21. What "surprise team" took I.U. out of the 1986 NCAA tournament?

22. Where was this game played?

23. Where were the first two of I.U.'s 1987 NCAA tournament games played?

Postseason Tournaments—Questions

24. What postseason tournament did I.U. play in in 1985?

25. Who beat I.U. in this tournament final and what was the score?

26. Indiana played how many games in this tournament?

27. Where were each of the games played?

28. Who did I.U. beat in double overtime in this tournament's quarterfinals?

29. What I.U. player, in the first overtime period, tied the score of this game with a free throw with no time remaining on the clock?

30. What team did I.U. beat in postseason tournament play in both 1984 and 1985?

31. In the opening round of the 1983 NCAA tournament, I.U. beat a team whose best player later played for Coach Knight on the U.S. Olympic team of 1984. Can you remember the team and the player?

32. In the opening round of the 1982 NCAA tournament, I.U. beat a small school located in the downtown area of Pittsburgh. Can you identify the school?

33. Where was this game played?

Postseason Tournaments—Questions

34. Who did I.U. lose to in the next round?

35. Why was this game sweet revenge for the winner?

36. Where was the 1981 NCAA Mideast Regional played?

37. What team did I.U. beat to go to the final four in 1981?

38. To open the 1981 NCAA tourney, Indiana defeated an ACC team at Dayton, Ohio. Which team?

39. This game featured I.U.'s running game, with which player tying an I.U. record for assists in a single game?

40. The team also broke two other team records in that game. Do you know them?

41. What is the modern I.U. record for points scored by them in an NCAA game?

42. True or false: I.U. trailed LSU at halftime in the 1981 semifinal NCAA tourney game.

43. Two Indiana ballplayers were named Most Outstanding Players for this game. Who were they?

Postseason Tournaments—Questions

44. Whose basket at the first-half buzzer gave I.U. its first lead in the final game of the 1981 national tournament?

45. Who was holding the ball for I.U. when the final buzzer went off in 1981 to give them their fourth national championship?

46. Name the three I.U. ballplayers named to the all-tournament team in the NCAA finals of 1981.

47. Who was named Most Valuable Player in the 1981 NCAA tournament?

48. Which of the players in question 46 was normally not a starter?

49. In the 1980 NCAA tournament, I.U. won in the opening round. Who did they beat?

50. Where was this game played?

51. Purdue took I.U. out of the 1980 NCAA regionals in the first game at what playing site?

52. What team did I.U. beat to win the NIT championship at Madison Square Garden in 1979?

53. Who made the winning basket for I.U. with seconds to go in that game?

Postseason Tournaments—Questions

54. Why were the NIT finals of 1979 nearly an "in-house" Big Ten affair?

55. Which Big Ten team did Indiana beat in the semifinal round of that tourney?

56. Indiana won away from home to open that NIT tourney against whom?

57. Before going to Madison Square Garden, I.U. had to defeat a little-known team with a 28-0 record at Assembly Hall in the second round. Who was this?

58. Coach Knight considered the NIT championship a big one. How many times had he been there before 1979?

59. What Big East team did I.U. lose to in the first game of the 1978 East Regional NCAA?

60. Whom had I.U. beaten in the first round to play this team?

61. In I.U.'s national championship tournament win of 1976, who gave them the closest game?

62. What Indiana players made the 1979 all-tournament NIT Team?

63. Who was selected MVP for this tournament?

Postseason Tournaments—Questions

64. Who were the four teams other than Alabama that Indiana defeated to win the NCAA 1976 tournament?

65. What Indiana ballplayers were on this 1976 NCAA Finals all-tournament team?

66. Who was selected Most Valuable Player?

67. Who beat I.U. in the first game of the 1972 NIT (Coach Knight's first year as Hoosier coach)?

68. What All-American center played on the team that beat I.U. in the 1973 NCAA semifinal game?

69. Who was I.U.'s All-American center who fouled out guarding him in that game?

70. Indiana beat what team in the consolation game for third place?

71. Where did I.U. play in the regional that year?

72. They beat two well-regarded teams in the regional to make the final four. Who were they?

73. What team did I.U. beat in the final game of the 1974 CCA tourney?

Postseason Tournaments—Questions

74. What two teams did I.U. defeat to move to the 1974 CCA final game?

75. Where did Indiana beat Texas El Paso in the opening round of the NCAA tournament in 1975?

76. Due to an NCAA ruling, how many players was Coach McCracken limited to in the NCAA tourney of 1940?

77. How many regionals did the 1940 NCAA tourney contain?

78. Only two teams went to the NCAA finals in 1940. How was the country divided for east and west regionals?

79. In 1940 Indiana won the East Regional at which location?

80. What two teams did they beat in the 1940 regional?

81. Who was MVP in the 1940 NCAA finals?

82. Who were the three I.U. players named to the all-tournament team?

83. What two teams did I.U. defeat in the NCAA regional in 1953?

84. Where was this regional played?

Postseason Tournaments—Questions

85. True or False: The NCAA tourney in 1953 consisted of more than 16 teams.

86. Who coached DePaul in the 1953 season?

87. Who did I.U. defeat in the semifinal round of the 1953 national tourney?

88. This team had a big, dominant center who later made a very good NBA player. Who was he?

89. Who was the most valuable player of the NCAA finals of 1953?
    a) Don Schlundt (I.U.)
    b) Bob Petit (LSU)
    c) B.H. Born (Kansas)
    d) Bob Leonard (I.U.)

90. Don Schlundt's 41 points against Notre Dame in the 1953 regional broke what former DePaul great's Chicago Stadium record of 37 points in a game?

91. What two I.U. players made the 1953 NCAA finals all-tournament team?

92. Who was Kansas's coach that year?

93. What team did I.U. beat in the consolation game of the 1967 NCAA regional?

Postseason Tournaments—Questions

94. Where was the 1974 CCA tournament played?

95. Where did I.U. play in the semifinal game of the 1973 NCAA tournament?

96. Who on I.U.'s team fouled out at 7:57 left in the second half of that game, severely hurting their chances of winning?

97. Scott May played how many minutes in Indiana's regional final against Kentucky in the 1975 NCAA tournament?
    a) 20½ minutes
    b) 7½ minutes
    c) 28½ minutes
    d) 14½ minutes

98. Indiana won NCAA tournaments with both the worst and best overall records in the history of the tournament. True or False?

99. What were the years and the records?

100. If Indiana's undefeated team had won their NCAA regional in 1975, what city would they have gone to for the final four?

101. The 1974 CCA tournament was the first ever held. Was there a second?

102. Who represented the Big Ten in that tournament?

Postseason Tournaments—Questions

103. Of Indiana's last 15 points in the final NCAA 1987 game against Syracuse, Keith Smart made ____ of them.
    a) 6
    b) 9
    c) 12
    d) 15

104. Which Indiana 1987 NCAA tournament game nearly got out of hand physically with the officials separating and warning players?

105. Which Indiana player was MVP of the 1973 Mideast Regional in the NCAA tournament?

106. What world leader died the day Indiana's invitation to the 1953 NCAA was announced?

107. Why did the Indianapolis Ministerial Association protest holding the 1940 Eastern NCAA Regional in their city?

108. What scorer's decision did Branch McCracken protest vehemently in the final game of the 1953 NCAA tourney?

109. Who was I.U.'s leading scorer in the 1987 final NCAA tournament game against Syracuse?

Postseason Tournaments—Questions

110. Who was the first Knight-era I.U. player awarded a technical foul? It happened late in the first half of I.U.'s final game of the 1974 CCA tournament.

111. Where was Coach Knight at this time?

112. Why was he there?

113. Who was the other member of the NCAA 1981 final four, defeated by fellow ACC member North Carolina in a semifinal game?

114. This Indiana player passed the ball to Keith Smart for the winning field goal in the 1987 NCAA final game. Who is he?

115. Where did Indiana play in the 1958 NCAA regionals?

116. Who did I.U. beat in the consolation game of the 1958 NCAA regionals?

117. Where did I.U. play the '67 NCAA Mideast Regional?

118. Name the usual starters on Indiana's 1967 team.

119. With injuries and dismissals the 1979 team was severely undermanned. How

Postseason Tournaments—Questions

many I.U. players suited up for the final NIT game?

120. Who in the 1987 NCAA tournament game against UNLV took a long defensive rebound the length of the floor for a three-point play (field goal and free throw) to give the Hoosiers a nine-point lead with 13 seconds to go?

121. In which 1987 NCAA tournament game were the Hoosiers down nine points with just over four minutes to play?

122. What I.U. ballplayer completed a three-point play to bring Indiana to within four points near the end of that game?

123. Who scored the final point for I.U. in their 69-68 victory over Kansas in the 1953 national championship game?

124. Indiana University has been taken out of the NCAA tournament four times by teams they beat earlier in the season. Can you name those teams and the years they accomplished that feat?

125. A former coach and close friend of Coach Knight lost to the Hoosiers by nine points in the NCAA regional final in 1976. He came back in 1977 to win the NCAA. Can you identify him and his team?

Postseason Tournaments—Questions

126. True or False: The I.U. basketball team made a short stop at Terre Haute's Hulman Field on the return flight from the NCAA finals in Kansas City in 1953.

Answers

1. UCLA (70-59)

2. I.U. defeated UCLA by 20 points (84-64) in the opening game of the 1976 season in St. Louis Arena.

3. The McCracken Memorial Floor was transported to St. Louis and reassembled there for the game.

4. Kentucky, in the regional finals at Dayton, Ohio

5. Scott May's broken arm

6. 92-90

Postseason Tournaments—Answers

7. I.U. won, 98-74.

8. Kentucky and Notre Dame

9. Kentucky in 1975 and 1983; Notre Dame in 1954 and 1958

10. North Carolina, 72-68

11. Virginia, 50-48

12. 6 times: 1940, 1953, 1973, 1976, 1981 and 1987

13. 1981—Isiah Thomas and Jim Thomas

14. Steve Alford and Keith Smart

15. Keith Smart

16. Rick Calloway broke his wrist only 14 minutes into the first half.

17. Both were injured and left the game in the first half, neither player scored, and both young men wore the number 20.

18. b

19. Fairfield, 92-58, Auburn, 107-90, Duke, 88-82, LSU, 77-76, UNLV, 97-93, and Syracuse, 74-73

20. LSU—four times

Postseason Tournaments—Answers

21. Cleveland State, 83-79

22. The Carrier Dome in Syracuse, New York

23. The Hoosier Dome in Indianapolis, Indiana

24. The NIT

25. UCLA, 65-62

26. Five

27. The first three at Assembly Hall and the last two at Madison Square Garden in New York

28. Marquette, 94-82

29. Uwe Blab

30. Richmond in the first round of the NCAA in 1984 (75-67) and again in the second round of the NIT in 1985 (75-53)

31. They beat Oklahoma, 63-49, with Wayman Tisdale as its standout.

32. Robert Morris College (94-62)

33. Vanderbilt University's Memorial Gymnasium in Nashville, Tennessee

Postseason Tournaments—Answers

34. University of Alabama at Birmingham (80-70)

35. I.U. had taken them out of the 1981 NCAA tourney, 87-72, in the opener of the Mideast Regional.

36. Assembly Hall at I.U.

37. St. Joseph's of Philadelphia

38. Maryland (99-64)

39. Isiah Thomas with 14

40. Points in an NCAA game (99) and shooting percentage in an NCAA game (.651)

41. 107 against Auburn in 1987

42. True (30-27)

43. Jim Thomas, who replaced Isiah Thomas when he picked up his fourth foul with 16:33 to go, and Landon Turner, who led all scorers with 20 points

44. Randy Wittman's

45. Isiah Thomas

46. Isiah Thomas, Jim Thomas and Landon Turner

Postseason Tournaments—Answers

47. Isiah Thomas

48. Jim Thomas

49. Virginia Tech (68-59)

50. At Western Kentucky University in Bowling Green, Kentucky

51. Rupp Arena, Lexington, Kentucky

52. Purdue (53-52)

53. Butch Carter

54. Three of the final four were Big Ten teams.

55. Ohio State (64-55)

56. Texas Tech (78-59)

57. Alcorn State (73-69)

58. Five: four times at Army and once at Indiana in the 1972 season, his first with the Hoosiers

59. Villanova (61-60)

60. Furman (63-62)

61. Alabama (74-69)

Postseason Tournaments—Answers

62. Mike Woodson, Ray Tolbert and Butch Carter

63. Butch Carter and Ray Tolbert were co-MVPs.

64. St. John's (90-70), Marquette (65-56), UCLA (65-51) and Michigan (86-68)

65. Scott May, Kent Benson and Tom Abernethy

66. Kent Benson

67. Princeton (68-60)

68. Bill Walton of UCLA

69. Steve Downing

70. Providence (97-79)

71. Vanderbilt in Nashville, Tennessee

72. Marquette (75-69) and Kentucky (72-65)

73. USC (85-60)

74. Tennessee (73-71) and Toledo in overtime (73-72)

75. Rupp Arena in Lexington, Kentucky

76. Ten

Postseason Tournaments—Answers

77. Two four-team regionals, east and west

78. The Mississippi River was the dividing line.

79. Butler Fieldhouse at Indianapolis, Indiana

80. Springfield and Duquesne

81. Marvin Huffman

82. Besides Huffman, Jay McCreary and Bill Menke

83. DePaul and Notre Dame

84. Chicago Stadium, Chicago, Illinois

85. True. Twenty-two teams started; six pre-regional games reduced the field to sixteen teams; Indiana had a first-round bye.

86. Ray Meyer

87. LSU

88. Bob Petit

89. c

90. George Mikan

91. Don Schlundt and Bob Leonard

92. Phog Allen

81

Postseason Tournaments—Answers

93. Tennessee (51-44)

94. St. Louis Arena, St. Louis, Missouri

95. St. Louis Arena, St. Louis, Missouri

96. Steve Downing

97. b

98. True

99. The 1976 team tied North Carolina's 1957 record for an NCAA champion at 32-0. The 1981 team set the record for the worst overall record at 27-9.

100. San Diego

101. Yes—in 1975 at Louisville, referred to as the National Commissioners Invitational Tournament

102. Purdue

103. c

104. The Auburn game

105. Steve Downing

106. Joseph Stalin

Postseason Tournaments—Answers

107. It was played on Good Friday (March 22) and Holy Saturday (March 23).

108. B.H. Born was charged with a fifth foul late in the third quarter, but the scorer changed it when press and radio men backed his coach's contention it was only his fourth.

109. Steve Alford, with 23

110. Steve Green

111. Watching the game from the stands

112. He received three technicals and was put out of the game with nine minutes left in the first half.

113. Virginia

114. Daryl Thomas

115. Lexington, Kentucky at the University of Kentucky Fieldhouse

116. Miami (Ohio)

117. Evanston, Illinois, at McGaw Hall

118. Butch Joyner, Jack Johnson, Bill DeHeer, Vern Payne and Bill Russell

Postseason Tournaments—Answers

119. Eight

120. Steve Eyl

121. The LSU game for the regional championship

122. Joe Hillman

123. Bob Leonard

124. Notre Dame in 1954, Purdue in 1980 and Kentucky in both 1975 and 1983

125. Al McGuire of Marquette

126. True

Big Ten General Trivia

1. Fill in the Big Ten university with the facility its basketball team uses for home games:
   a) _____ Field House (1930)
   b) _____ Assembly Hall (1971)
   c) _____ Jenison Field House (1939)
   d) _____ William's Arena (1928)
   e) _____ Welsh-Ryan Arena (1951)
   f) _____ Mackey Arena (1967)
   g) _____ Carver-_____ Sports Arena (1983)
   h) _____ St. John's Arena (1957)
   i) _____ Assembly Hall (1963)
   j) _____ Crisler Arena (1967)

Big Ten General Trivia—Questions

2. Name the head basketball coach at each Big Ten school:
   a) Illinois
   b) Indiana
   c) Iowa
   d) Michigan
   e) Michigan State
   f) Minnesota
   g) Northwestern
   h) Ohio State
   i) Purdue
   j) Wisconsin

3. The forerunner of the Big Ten started in what year as the "Intercollegiate Conference of Faculty Representatives"?

4. When did Indiana University join this organization?

5. Of the original Big Ten, one university withdrew in 1946. Which one?

6. Who replaced them in 1949?

7. Which present Big Ten head basketball coach has coached the longest in the conference?

8. Which home basketball facility has the largest seating capacity?

9. Who is the present head coach in the Big Ten with the second longest tenure?

Big Ten General Trivia—Questions

10. Who is third in this category?

11. In the 1987 season the Big Ten had four "freshman" coaches. Can you name them?

12. What current Big Ten head coach has the greatest number of collegiate-level victories?

13. How many NCAA tournaments have Big Ten teams won in the 48 years of the history of the tournament?

14. Indiana has five championships; what teams have the others?

15. Who is the present commissioner of the Big Ten?

16. Who was the Big Ten Newcomer of the Year for the 1987 season?

17. What Big Ten team has the best won-lost percentage in NCAA tournament play?

18. Where is the Big Ten conference office?

19. Identify the close friend of Coach Knight's who is a retired Big Ten basketball official from Terre Haute, Indiana.

Answers

1. a) Wisconsin's
   b) Indiana's
   c) Michigan State's
   d) Minnesota's
   e) Northwestern's
   f) Purdue's
   g) Iowa's Hawkeye
   h) Ohio State's
   i) Illinois'
   j) Michigan's

2. a) Lou Henson
   b) Bob Knight
   c) Tom Davis
   d) Bill Frieder
   e) Jud Heathcote
   f) Clem Haskins
   g) Bill Foster
   h) Gary Williams
   i) Gene Keady
   j) Steve Yoder

3. 1896

4. 1899

5. Chicago University

Big Ten General Trivia—Answers

6. Michigan State

7. Bob Knight (16 years)

8. Indiana University's Assembly Hall—17,357

9. Lou Henson of Illinois (12 years)

10. Jud Heathcote of Michigan State (11 years)

11. Tom Davis of Iowa, Clem Haskins of Minnesota, Bill Foster of Northwestern and Gary Williams of Ohio State

12. If you said Coach Knight, you're wrong. It's Lou Henson with 481!

13. Eight

14. Wisconsin in 1941, Ohio State in 1960 and Michigan State in 1979

15. Wayne Duke

16. Dean Garrett

17. Wisconsin, 4-1 for an .800 percentage (1941-47)

18. Schaumburg, Illinois

19. Charlie Fouty

Holiday Tournaments

1. How many years has the Indiana Classic been held?
    a) 9
    b) 15
    c) 11
    d) 13

2. How many of these tournaments have had an I.U. player as MVP?
    a) All of them
    b) All but three
    c) All but two
    d) All but one

3. Who was the Most Valuable Player in the 1987-season Indiana Classic?

Holiday Tournaments—Questions

4. Who is the only I.U. ballplayer to make the All-Indiana Classic team four times?

5. Two I.U. ballplayers have been MVPs in the Indiana Classic twice. Which two?
   a) Kent Benson 1976 and 1977
   b) Mike Woodson 1979 and 1980
   c) Randy Wittman 1982 and 1983
   d) Uwe Blab 1984 and 1985

6. Of the following eleven players, seven have made the All-Indiana Classic team each year they have played. Can you identify them?
   a) Steve Green
   b) Quinn Buckner
   c) Scott May
   d) Kent Benson
   e) Mike Woodson
   f) Wayne Radford
   g) Landon Turner
   h) Isiah Thomas
   i) Uwe Blab
   j) Steve Alford
   k) Marty Simmons

7. How many years has the Hoosier Classic been held?
   a) One
   b) Seven
   c) Three
   d) Five

8. Where is the Hoosier Classic held?

9. Has Indiana ever lost either an Indiana Classic or a Hoosier Classic?

Holiday Tournaments—Questions

10. The first year of the Hoosier Classic, Cornell was coached by what Knight former assistant?

11. Who did Coach Knight coach against, also a former assistant coach, in the 1987-season Hoosier Classic?

12. Has a Knight-coached I.U. team ever played in the New Orleans' Superdome before the NCAA final four in 1987?

13. In the Knight era, I.U. has played in how many Holiday Classic tournaments other than the Indiana and Hoosier Classics?
    a) 4
    b) 8
    c) 12
    d) 16

14. What is the last invitational classic tournament a Knight-coached I.U. team played in other than the Indiana or Hoosier Classic?

15. Name the cities where Indiana played the following invitational tournaments:
    a) Old Dominion Classic
    b) Sun Bowl Classic
    c) Far West Classic
    d) Rainbow Classic
    e) The Holiday Festival
    f) Gator Bowl Classic
    g) Seawolf Classic
    h) Cabrillo Classic

16. In the 1979 season I.U. played in two invitational classics outside the state of Indiana. What were they?

Holiday Tournaments—Questions

17. How many of the Knight-era invitational classics other than the Indiana Classic or the Hoosier Classic has I.U. won?

18. Which three out-of-state invitational classics did Knight-era I.U. teams play in twice?

19. What out-of-state invitational classic in the Knight era did I.U. make the worst showing in?
    a) 1977 Sugar Bowl
    b) 1982 Holiday Festival
    c) 1981 Rainbow Classic
    d) 1979 Seawolf Classic

20. Who was the Most Valuable Player in the 1980 Cabrillo Classic?
    a) Mike Woodson
    b) Ray Tolbert
    c) Isiah Thomas

21. What two teams beat I.U. in the 1981 Rainbow Classic?

22. In a field of eight, what was I.U.'s position finish in the 1979 Seawolf Classic?
    a) First
    b) Third
    c) Fifth
    d) Seventh

Holiday Tournaments—Questions

23. Which five of the following Knight-era invitational classics did I.U. win?
    a) The Old Dominion Classic of 1972
    b) The Sun Bowl Classic of 1973
    c) The Far West Classic of 1974
    d) The Rainbow Classic of 1975
    e) The Holiday Festival of 1976
    f) The Gator Bowl Classic of 1978
    g) The Cabrillo Classic of 1980

Answers

1. d

2. d

3. Brian Rowsome of UNC/Wilmington

4. Mike Woodson (1977-1980)

5. b and d

6. a, b, c, d, e, h and k

7. d

8. Market Square Arena in Indianapolis, Indiana

Holiday Tournaments—Answers

9. No

10. Tom Miller

11. Bob Donewald, Illinois State

12. Yes—they played the Sugar Bowl Classic there in the 1977 season.

13. c

14. The Holiday Festival (1982)

15. a) Norfolk   e) New York City
    b) El Paso   f) Jacksonville
    c) Portland   g) Anchorage
    d) Honolulu   h) San Diego

16. The Seawolf Classic and the Far West Classic

17. Five

18. The Far West Classic (1974 and 1979)
    The Rainbow Classic (1975 and 1981)
    The Holiday Festival (1976 and 1982)

19. b—they were fourth in a field of four.

20. c

21. Clemson and Pan American

Holiday Tournaments—Answers

22. d

23. a, d, e, f and g

Players

1. Name the most recent Knight-era I.U. MVP, first-team Big Ten, Academic All-American and Academic All Big Ten who is a Phi Beta Kappa.

2. Who was the leading scorer in the Big Ten in 1953?

3. Who was the leading scorer in the Big Ten in 1957?

4. Identify the five usual starters on the 1957 I.U. Big Ten co-championship team.

5. Who were the usual starters on the 1958 NCAA team?

6. Who does Coach Knight consider his first recruit while at I.U.?

7. The team captain for I.U.'s 1987 team was _____.
    a) Steve Alford
    b) Daryl Thomas
    c) Todd Meier
    d) All of the above

8. Who led the I.U. team in rebounding in 1987?

9. The leader in assists for the 1987 team was who?

10. I.U. played 127 basketball games during Steve Alford's career. How many starts did he have?
    a) 127
    b) 124
    c) 120
    d) 117

11. Can you recall two games that Alford did not play in at all?

12. Can you identify the I.U. player who played only the 1986 season but was the team's leading rebounder that year?

13. What I.U. player led the team in rebounding, both in his junior year in 1984 and his senior year in 1985?

Players—Questions

14. Who led I.U. in rebounding in 1982 and 1983?

15. What I.U. player has an Olympic Gold Medal, an NCAA championship ring and an NBA championship ring but never played in an NBA All-Star game?

16. Bob Knight era players who play out their eligibility have about a 93 percent rate of receiving I.U. degrees. Can you name two who did not play out their eligibility but still have I.U. degrees?

17. In 42 years of selection, the Big Ten's MVP Award often went to I.U. players. What two players each won the award twice?

18. Name an I.U. player who played on an NCAA championship team and later coached an Indiana high school team to a state championship and a state runner-up.

19. What I.U. player suffered an injury in the NCAA final game in 1976?

20. What was the nature of his injury?

21. Who replaced him in that game and played well?

22. Who in the 1974 and 1975 seasons was known as the Super-sub?

103

Players—Questions

23. What two I.U. players were on Denny Crum's Pan-Am Games team of 1987?

24. What third member of the I.U. team tried out for this team and wasn't selected?

25. What I.U. ballplayer is credited with doing a great job defensively on Michael Jordan of North Carolina in the 1984 NCAA regional?

26. Who captained the 1982 Hoosiers?

27. Can you identify a Knight-era I.U. center and an All-American McCracken-era I.U. center with the same last names?

28. Can you name a player who was named MVP for the Indiana team four times?

29. What two players, named I.U. MVP three times each, did he pass?

30. Alford shared the I.U. MVP award in 1985 with which player?

31. Where did Indiana play the 1987 NCAA regional?

32. Who made the winning basket against LSU in the regional final there?

33. Whose missed air-ball shot did he rebound to score this winning basket?

Players—Questions

34. Although they played only part of the 1956 season, these two Chicago-area players were very exciting to watch. Who were they?

35. What were their nicknames?

36. Who was a good I.U. forward from Attica, Indiana, who died in an auto accident around Memorial Day 1950?

37. Who was known as the "Splendid Splinter"? He was an I.U. scoring champ, an All-American and played from the 1961 through the 1963 seasons.

38. Where was he from?

39. An old adversary from high school days of the above ballplayer, he played at I.U. in the 1961 season, roomed with the above player, but was paralyzed in a 1961 auto accident. Who was he?

40. Where was he from?

41. Who was known as the "People's Choice" when he played at I.U.?

42. Where was he from?

43. When the Big Ten adopted the three-point basket for the 1983 season, Coach Knight

Players—Questions

said, "That's all right with me. There are three kids in the conference who can hit that shot and I have two of them." To whom was he referring?

44. Who was the third kid he referred to?

45. Although he played at I.U. only one year, his average points per game for that year is the highest in I.U. history. Who is he?

46. A high school teammate of his went on to become a Big Ten MVP and All-American at I.U. Who was he?

47. Two I.U. Big Ten Most Valuable Players wore the same number. Can you identify them?

48. What was the number?

49. Two I.U. Big Ten Most Valuable Players didn't make All-Big Ten the years they were MVP. Who were they?

50. He played at I.U. for Branch McCracken from 1949 through 1951; he is a high school coach and has, in the past ten years, sent three players to Coach Knight's program (one an Indiana high school Mr. Basketball). Can you name this high school coach who is a former player?

Players—Questions

51. What high school does he coach?

52. Who were the three players referred to in question 50?

53. Between them, two of these three players led I.U. in assists three consecutive years. Can you identify them and the years?

54. In 42 years of selecting Big Ten Most Valuable Players, how many times has an I.U. player been selected?
    a) 14
    b) 11
    c) 8
    d) 5

55. How many of these have been Knight-era Big Ten MVP selections?

56. Who was Indiana's first Big Ten MVP?

57. Who is I.U.'s most recent Big Ten MVP?

58. A four-year starter at I.U., he spent most of his last season recovering from back surgery but nevertheless was selected Big Ten MVP. Can you identify the player and the season?

59. What I.U. captain of 1958, now a Lebanon, Indiana attorney, recently was presi-

Players—Questions

dent of the Varsity Club National board of directors?

60. What two Knight-era players, both Indiana high school Mr. Basketballers and four-year I.U. starters, were Big Ten MVPs?

61. An associate director of athletics at I.U., Knight-era All-American, I.U.'s leading rebounder two years (junior and senior), and leading scorer his senior year, was also selected Big Ten MVP. Who is he and what was the year of his selection?

62. Who led the Hoosiers in rebounding in 1971?

63. Since 1979 three players came to the I.U. program from St. Joseph's High School in Westchester, Illinois. Can you name them?

64. Who coached these three in high school?

65. High school coach Howard Sharpe, the winningest coach in Indiana high school history, coached Bob Leonard at Terre Haute Gerstmeyer. He also sent another player to Coach McCracken who captained and was the leading rebounder of the 1962 team. Who was he?

66. Who was I.U.'s leading scorer in 1962?

Players—Questions

67. Indiana's MVP, team captain, and All-Big Ten in 1963 has a son who has just entered I.U.'s football program. Can you identify him?

68. In 1983 this player was team MVP, co-captain, leading scorer, All-Big Ten, All-American and a Big Ten MVP. Who is he?

69. The other 1983 co-captain was leading scorer and MVP in 1982, All-Big Ten in 1982 and 1983 and All-American in 1982 and 1983. Who is he?

70. Who are the four I.U. players with Olympic gold medals?

71. What I.U. ballplayer was selected for the Olympic team but never participated in the games?

72. What I.U. player was the team captain of an Olympic team?

73. Can you think of another I.U. player who competed in the Olympics?

74. Playing on Coach Knight's 1979 USA Pan-Am Games team were three I.U. players. Name them.

75. Which I.U. player co-captained this team?

109

Players—Questions

76. What I.U. player, who transferred before his eligibility was over, appeared in the 1987 final four with another team?

77. Can you recall another I.U. ballplayer who transferred away after winning an NCAA championship ring and appeared later in the final four of an NCAA tournament with another team?

78. Prior to the 1987 first- and second-round NCAA tournament games played at the Hoosier Dome in Indianapolis, Indiana, only one college basketball player had any experience playing there. Can you think of who this would have been?

79. Of the 44 Knight-era I.U. players who played out their eligibility, how many have graduate degrees as of the summer of 1986?

80. What Knight-era All-American was a non-predictor but now has two degrees?

81. There are two attorneys from the Class of 1981 who were former I.U. players. Do you know them?

82. There are two orthopedic surgeons, former I.U. Knight-era players, now practicing in Indianapolis. Name them.

Players—Questions

83. What 1975 All-American I.U. player now practices dentistry in Indianapolis?

84. Who served as chief medical officer for basketball during this summer's Pan-Am Games in Indianapolis?

85. What was the song played by the pep band during the 1973 season and through the 1976 season as a tribute to one of I.U.'s players?

86. What important player and captain of the 1973 team was an Academic All-Big Ten three years and an Academic All-American in 1973?

87. Who was the leading rebounder on I.U.'s 1953 team?

88. What I.U. ballplayer's father played on the only unbeaten I.U. football team and only uncontested conference champion?

89. What two starters from I.U.'s 1953 team have passed away?

90. Who was I.U.'s consensus College Player of the Year?

91. How many years did Quinn Buckner play football at I.U.?

92. What game marked John Laskowski's first

Players—Questions

   start with I.U.'s team?
   a) The 1975 Purdue game at home
   b) The 1975 Purdue game away
   c) The 1974 first CCA game against Tennessee

93. Which starting guard did Laz replace in this start?
    a) Quinn Buckner
    b) Bobby Wilkerson
    c) Steve Ahlfeld

94. How many minutes did Laz play in this game?
    a) 40
    b) 35
    c) 25

95. Who paid for Scott May's first year at I.U.?

96. Following is a list of player nicknames. Can you match them with the players' real names?

    a) Spiderman
    b) Tex
    c) Bubbles
    d) Cam
    e) Bootsie
    f) Butch
    g) Curly

    1. Paul C. Armstrong
    2. Robert E. Armstrong
    3. Malcolm Cameron
    4. Jack Campbell
    5. Gary A. Grieger
    6. Andre Harris
    7. James H. Harris
    8. Harry C. Joyner
    9. Donald E. Ritter
    10. John P. Ritter
    11. Cornelius White
    12. Richard E. White
    13. Bobby Wilkerson
    14. Robert E. Wilkinson

Players—Questions

97. There were three early-round draft choices in the NBA from McCracken's 1965 team who made very durable pros (playing 35 pro seasons between them). Name the players.

98. Who were the co-captains of this 1965 team?

99. Name the leading scorer on the 1963 team when Jon McGlocklin and the "Vans" were sophomores.

100. In winning UPI's James A. Naismith award for College Player of the Year in 1976, Scott May beat what in-state player by two votes?

101. This Indiana native and 1981 player for I.U. is now a salesman for Chas. Pfizer Inc. He was usually used in a reserve role and moved well without the ball. He often became open along the baseline. Can you identify him?

102. In the 1976 season, Indiana won an overtime game against which Big Ten team at home?

103. Who tipped the ball in the basket as time ran out to put the game in overtime?

104. Just prior to that tip-in, who batted a long rebound back toward the basket to keep it in play?

Players—Questions

105. What player took the final shot that gave the long rebound that started that final sequence?

106. In that same 1976 season, what other team took Indiana into an overtime before losing 77-68 to them?

107. Who tipped in a blocked shot with nine seconds to go to tie that game?

108. Whose blocked shot did he tip?

109. In I.U.'s triple-overtime game at Wisconsin in 1987, who rebounded an air-ball shot and put it in the hoop with three seconds to go in the third overtime to win the game, 86-85?

110. Who shot the air-ball that he rebounded?

111. What I.U. player was dropped from the team in the 1987 season for academic reasons and was reinstated on a probationary status three days later?

112. Besides I.U.'s three seniors, one other player from the 1987 season will be missing from the 1988 team. Who is he?

113. Can you come close to the percentage of total 1987 season I.U. points that the above four players accounted for?

Players—Questions

114. In 1986 Steve Alford was one of three captains of the I.U. team. Who were the other two?

115. Who captained the Hoosiers in both Alford's freshman and sophomore years?

116. Which arm did Scott May break in the 1975 season?

117. Can you recall four I.U. All-Americans from Newcastle, Indiana?

118. Do you recall a player from Newcastle who scored over a thousand points in his I.U. career from 1966 to 1968, was I.U.'s MVP and All-Big Ten in 1967 and team captain in 1968?

119. What was John Laskowski's first start in Assembly Hall?
    a) against Purdue in 1975
    b) against Ohio State in 1975
    c) against Michigan in 1975

120. Identify the Indiana high school Mr. Basketball from Lafayette Jeff who captained the Hoosiers in 1952.

121. Identify the Indiana High School Mr. Basketball from the 1953 Indianapolis Crispus Attucks' team who played guard at I.U. from 1955 to 1957. He wore number 21.

Players—Questions

122. Identify the Indiana high school Mr. Basketball for 1979 from Washington, Indiana, who wore number 54 and played four years at I.U.

123. This player wore number 23, played at I.U. from 1966 to 1968, was I.U.'s leading scorer and MVP in 1968. Can you name him?

124. This man played at Indiana 1967-1969, wore number 31, led the team in rebounding in 1968 and captained the team in 1969. Can you identify this player?

125. This player of 1968-1970, wore number 22, led the Hoosiers in scoring in 1969 and joined the "over 1,000 career points club" with 1,099. Who is he?

126. This player played in 1970-1971 wearing number 30. He was the Most Valuable Player and leading scorer in 1970, and team captain in 1971. Can you identify him?

127. Two players, both wearing number 33, one playing from 1965-1967 and the other from 1968-1970, had the same last name. Can you name the player who captained I.U. in 1967?

128. Can you name the player who was the leading rebounder in 1969 and 1970 and MVP in 1969?

Players—Questions

129. Max Walker (1964-1966) was the leading scorer, MVP, and captain of the I.U. 1966 team. True or false.

130. Which member of the 1987 I.U. team also stars in the outfield on the I.U. baseball team?

131. Who was the first junior-college player to play for Coach Knight?

132. What were this player's family ties to the I.U. basketball program?

133. How many junior-college players has Coach Knight taken at I.U.?

134. How many of these players have not made it academically?

135. What three players were dismissed from the I.U. squad early in the 1979 season for violating training rules?

136. Identify an Indiana University baseball player who Coach Knight invited to join the 1979 team to help fill out the roster.

137. Why couldn't Mike Woodson be redshirted in the 1980 season when his back problem finally became severe enough to necessitate surgery?

117

Players—Questions

138. Name an I.U. player (1933-1935) who coached the undefeated Terre Haute Garfield High School team to the final game of the 1947 state tournament, only to be beaten by Shelbyville.

139. This Shelbyville team provided Indiana's high school Mr. Basketball for 1947, who later became an I.U. All-American. Who was he?

140. Which school did players Rick Rowray and Mike LaFave both transfer to?

141. Where did the following players transfer?
    a) Mike Giomi
    b) John Flowers
    c) Rich Valavicius
    d) Derek Holcomb

142. Name the best player ever to enroll at Indiana. He left after only a few weeks and later picked up his career at another university.

143. What is the one thing this player doesn't have that he would have had if he had stayed at I.U.?

144. This present I.U. player's father played at Evansville University, with the Chicago Bulls and later coached the Bulls. Who is this I.U. player?

Players—Questions

145. This I.U. player from 1980 to 1984 was the leading scorer in Indiana high school basketball for the 1979 season. Who is he?

146. This man was I.U.'s captain in 1951 and a scrappy ball player from Gary Froebel. Name him.

147. Why was Steve Alford suspended for a 1986-season game at Kentucky by the NCAA?

148. Which sorority put together this calendar?

149. How did the NCAA find out about this violation?

150. I.U.'s starting lineup in 1976 included four first-round NBA draft choices (three in 1976 and one in 1977) and a third-round 1976 draft choice. Can you sort them out?

151. Who from I.U. was drafted by the Boston Celtics in 1982?

152. Bob Leonard, who was on the 1953 national championship team, was from Terre Haute, Indiana. A second player on that same team was also from Terre Haute. Who was he?

Answers

1. Uwe Blab

2. Don Schlundt

3. Archie Dees

4. Dick Neal and Pete Obremsky at forwards, Archie Dees at center, and Hallie Bryant and Charlie Hodson at guards

5. Sam Gee, Archie Dees, Jerry Thompson, Pete Obremsky and Bob Wilkinson

6. Steve Green

7. d

Players—Answers

8. Dean Garrett with 288

9. Steve Alford with 123

10. c

11. The Kentucky game away in the 1986 season, due to an NCAA suspension, and the 1985 season Illinois game away.

12. Andre Harris with 162

13. Uwe Blab, 190 in 1984 and 207 in 1985

14. Jim Thomas, 181 in 1982 and 159 in 1983

15. Quinn Buckner

16. Isiah Thomas and Trent Smock

17. Archie Dees (1957-1958) and Scott May (1975-1976)

18. Jay McCreary coached Muncie Central to a championship in 1952 and runner-up in 1954. He also played for the I.U. NCAA champions in 1940.

19. Bob Wilkerson

20. Concussion

21. Jimmy Wisman

Players—Answers

22. John Laskowski

23. Dean Garrett and Keith Smart

24. Rick Calloway

25. Dan Dakich

26. Landon Turner

27. Dean Garrett and Bill Garrett

28. Steve Alford

29. Don Schlundt (1953, 1954, 1955) and Walt Bellamy (1959, 1960, 1961)

30. Uwe Blab

31. Riverfront Coliseum in Cincinnati, Ohio

32. Rick Calloway

33. Daryl Thomas

34. Charlie Brown and Pakstan Lumpkin

35. "Sweet Charlie" Brown and "Sugar" Lumpkin

36. Jerry Stuteville

37. Jimmy Rayl

Players—Answers

38. Kokomo, Indiana

39. Ray Pavy

40. Newcastle, Indiana

41. Wally Choice (1954-1956)

42. Montclair, New Jersey

43. He never said, but he must have been referring to Ted Kitchel and Randy Wittman.

44. No one knows. He may have been trying to psyche out the entire rosters of the other nine clubs.

45. George McGinnis, 29.9 in 1971

46. Steve Downing (1973)

47. Scott May (1975-1976) and Mike Woodson (1980)

48. Forty-two

49. Mike Woodson (1980) and Ray Tolbert (1981)

50. Phil Buck

51. Anderson Madison Heights

Players—Answers

52. Ray Tolbert, Winston Morgan and Stew Robinson

53. Stew Robinson, 104 in 1984 and 134 in 1985, and Winston Morgan, 133 in 1986

54. b

55. Eight

56. Don Schlundt (1953)

57. Steve Alford (1987)

58. Mike Woodson, 1980

59. Pete Obremsky

60. Kent Benson (1977) and Ray Tolbert (1981)

61. Steve Downing, 1973

62. George McGinnis with 352—he was Downing's high school classmate.

63. Isiah Thomas, Daryl Thomas and Tony Freeman

64. Gene Pingatore

65. Charley Hall

66. Jimmy Rayl

Players—Answers

67. Tom Bolyard

68. Randy Wittman

69. Ted Kitchel

70. Walt Bellamy (1960), Quinn Buckner and Scott May (1976), and Steve Alford (1984)

71. Isiah Thomas 1980. The USA did not attend the games in Moscow.

72. Quinn Buckner (1976)

73. Uwe Blab for West Germany in 1984

74. Isiah Thomas, Mike Woodson and Ray Tolbert

75. Mike Woodson

76. Delray Brooks, Providence (1987)

77. Bobby Bender, Duke (1978)

78. Steve Alford. In July of 1984, Steve played with the USA Olympic team there against a team of NBA All-Stars in an exhibition game.

79. Eight

Players—Answers

80. Steve Downing, B.S. and Masters in Physical Education

81. Glen Grunwald, practicing in Chicago and Phil Isenbarger, practicing in Indianapolis

82. Frank Wilson (1973) and Steve Ahlfeld (1975)

83. Steve Green

84. Steve Ahlfeld

85. "The Mighty Quinn"

86. John Ritter

87. Charley Kraak

88. Quinn Buckner's father Bill Buckner played on the Big Nine I.U. championship team in 1945. They were 9-0-1.

89. Don Schlundt and Dick Farley

90. Scott May in 1976. He won the James A. Naismith Trophy as UPI's College Player of the Year.

91. His first two

92. c

93. c

Players—Answers

94. a

95. Scott did, using a national defense loan. As an out-of-state non-predictor, he was not eligible for a Federal Economic Opportunity grant.

96. a) 13
    b) 9
    c) 7
    d) 3
    e) 11
    f) 8
    g) 1

97. Jon McGlocklin, Tom Van Arsdale and Dick Van Arsdale

98. Jon McGlocklin and Al Harden

99. Jimmy Rayl

100. Adrian Dantley of Notre Dame

101. Steve Risley

102. Michigan, 72-67

103. Kent Benson

104. Jim Crews

105. Quinn Buckner

Players—Answers

106. Kentucky

107. Kent Benson

108. Tom Abernethy

109. Dean Garrett

110. Joe Hillman

111. Daryl Thomas

112. Tony Freeman. He has transferred to Chicago State.

113. Forty-eight percent: Alford 749, Thomas 534, Freeman 35 and Meier 31, of a total 2,806 I.U. points

114. Winston Morgan and Stew Robinson

115. Dan Dakich

116. His left

117. Vern Huffman (1936), Marvin Huffman (1940), Kent Benson (1975-1977) and Steve Alford (1986-1987)

118. Butch Joyner

119. a

120. Bob Masters

Players—Answers

121. Hallie Bryant

122. Steve Bouchie

123. Vernon Payne

124. Bill DeHeer

125. Joe Cooke

126. James Harris

127. Jack Johnson

128. Ken Johnson

129. False. He was the leading scorer and MVP, but Gary Grieger captained the team.

130. Joe Hillman

131. Courtney Witte (1984-1986)

132. His father, Norbert Witte, played there for Coach McCracken in 1959 and 1960, and his uncle, Jerry Memering, played there for Coaches Watson and Knight from 1971 to 1973.

133. Six. Besides Witte, they are Todd Jadlow, Andre Harris, Keith Smart, Dean Garrett and Mark Robinson.

Players—Answers

134. Only one. Andre Harris left after his first year.

135. Jim Roberson, Tommy Baker and Don Cox

136. Steve Reish

137. He had already played in six games of the Hoosier's 27 scheduled games, over the prescribed 20 percent.

138. Willard Kehrt

139. Bill Garrett

140. Ball State University

141. a) North Carolina State
     b) UNLV
     c) Auburn
     d) Illinois

142. Larry Bird of Indiana State University

143. An NCAA championship ring. He would have been a member of I.U.'s 1976 team as a sophomore.

144. Brian Sloan, son of Jerry Sloan

145. Chuck Franz

146. Bill Tosheff

Players—Answers

147. He posed for a calendar sponsored by an I.U. sorority. It was put together to raise money for a summer camp it sponsored for handicapped girls.

148. Gamma Phi Beta

149. I.U. made them aware of it when the player, the coaches and the intercollegiate athletic department became aware that, technically, without intent, they had committed a violation of the NCAA rules.

150. Tom Abernethy (1976), third-round choice of Los Angeles; Kent Benson (1977), first-round choice of Milwaukee; Quinn Buckner (1976), first-round choice of Milwaukee; Scott May (1976), first-round choice of Chicago; Bob Wilkerson (1976), first-round choice of Seattle

151. Landon Turner

152. Dick White from Terre Haute Wiley

Numbers and Hometowns

Place the player's number and hometown after his name. One number may be used more than once! Hometowns you are on your own!

Numbers to be used: 11, 14, 15, 20, 22, 23, 25, 30, 31, 32, 33, 34, 35, 37, 40, 41, 42, 43, 44, 45, 50, 54.

1. Allen, Doug 1973-1976 ___ ___
2. Bouchie, Steve 1980-1983 ___ ___
3. Brown, Tony 1980-1983 ___ ___
4. Byers, Phil 1952, 1954-1955 ___ ___
5. Cameron, Malcolm 1982-1984 ___ ___
6. Eells, Scott 1976-1979 ___ ___
7. Foster, Tracy 1983 ___ ___
8. Franz, Chuck 1980-1984 ___ ___
9. Gee, Sam 1956-1958 ___ ___
10. Giomi, Mike 1983-1984 ___ ___
11. Grunwald, Glen 1977-1981 ___ ___

Numbers and Hometowns—Questions

12. Haymore, Mark 1975-1976 ____ _____
13. Hodson, Charles 1955-1956 ____ _____
14. Isenbarger, Phil 1978-1981 ____ _____
15. Jadlow, Todd 1986-1987 ____ _____
16. Kamstra, John 1973-1975 ____ _____
17. Kirchner, Eric 1978-1981 ____ _____
18. LaFave, Mike 1981-1982 ____ _____
19. Memering, Jerry 1971-1973 ____ _____
20. Mickey, Gordon E. 1960-1962 ____ _____
21. Minor, David 1987 ____ _____
22. Morris, Craig 1973-1974 ____ _____
23. Neal, Dick 1955-1957 ____ _____
24. Noort, Don 1973-1975 ____ _____
25. Oliphant, Jeff 1986-1987 ____ _____
26. Pelkowski, Magnus 1985-1987 ____ _____
27. Poff, Paul 1953-1957 ____ _____
28. Radford, Wayne 1975-1978 ____ _____
29. Radovich, Frank 1958-1960 ____ _____
30. Risley, Steve 1978-1981 ____ _____
31. Ritter, John 1971-1973 ____ _____
32. Russel, William 1965-1967 ____ _____
33. Scott, Burke 1953-1955 ____ _____
34. Simmons, Marty 1984-1985 ____ _____
35. Sloan, Brian 1985-1987 ____ _____
36. Smith, Kreigh 1985-1987 ____ _____
37. Thompson, Jerry 1956-1958 ____ _____
38. Valavicius, Richard 1976-1977 ____ _____
39. Wilson, Frank 1971-1973 ____ _____
40. Wisman, Jim 1975-1978 ____ _____

Answers

1. 25 Champaign, Illinois
2. 54 Washington, Indiana
3. 31 Chicago, Illinois
4. 14 Evansville, Indiana
5. 25 Terre Haute, Indiana
6. 31 Hoopeston, Illinois
7. 40 Fort Wayne, Indiana
8. 23 Clarksville, Indiana
9. 15 Washington, Indiana

Numbers and Hometowns—Answers

10.	41	Newark, Ohio
11.	40	Franklin Park, Illinois
12.	32	Shaker Heights, Ohio
13.	23	Muncie, Indiana
14.	44	Muncie, Indiana
15.	11	Salina, Kansas
16.	30	Rossville, Indiana
17.	33	Edelstein, Illinois
18.	43	Indianapolis, Indiana
19.	33	Vincennes, Indiana
20.	30	Chillicothe, Ohio
21.	31	Cincinnati, Ohio
22.	23	DeGraff, Ohio
23.	37	Reelsville, Indiana
24.	43	Chicago, Illinois
25.	35	Lyons, Indiana
26.	14	Bogata, Columbia

Numbers and Hometowns—Answers

27.	30	New Albany, Indiana
28.	22	Indianapolis, Indiana
29.	33	Hammond, Indiana
30.	34	Indianapolis, Indiana
31.	42	Goshen, Indiana
32.	22	Columbus, Indiana
33.	25	Tell City, Indiana
34.	50	Lawrenceville, Illinois
35.	45	McLeansboro, Illinois
36.	42	Tipton, Indiana
37.	45	South Bend, Indiana
38.	34	Hammond, Indiana
39.	20	Bluffton, Indiana
40.	23	Quincy, Illinois

Photographs

1. Identify this building.

Photographs—Questions

2. This structure is what?

Photographs—Questions

3. This building is just north of Assembly Hall's parking area. Identify it.

Photographs—Questions

4. Two buildings are built together here and are referred to now as the HPER Building. In the early fifties the peaked section to the left was known as what?

Photographs—Questions

5. This building, which was on the right in the previous photo, was known in the fifties as what?

143

Photographs—Questions

6. Identify this campus chapel.

144

Photographs—Questions

7. This little cemetery next to the chapel is very close to which large campus building?

Photographs—Questions

8. What is the name of this structure?

Photographs—Questions

9. Name this fountain and the building behind it.

Photographs—Questions

10. This street with the little circle in the center is what?

148

Photographs—Questions

11. Name this building.

Photographs—Questions

12. Identify this meadow and stream. In which direction does it flow, east to west or west to east?

Photographs—Questions

13. What is the structure centered in this picture?

Photographs—Questions

14. You can see the game on a large screen here and drown your troubles if the Hoosiers lose. It is _____.
    a) Dick's English Hut
    b) Mick's English Hut
    c) Nick's English Hut
    d) Rick's English Hut

Photographs—Questions

15. Now Garcia's Pizza, this structure was known as what in the fifties?

Photographs—Questions

16. Identify this building.

Photographs—Questions

17. What is this campus landmark?

Photographs—Questions

18. The old library pictured here is now

Photographs—Questions

19. This tower is part of which building?

Photographs—Questions

20. Identify this I.U. player.

Photographs—Questions

21. Identify the I.U. player in the center.

Photographs—Questions

22. Name this I.U. player.

Photographs—Questions

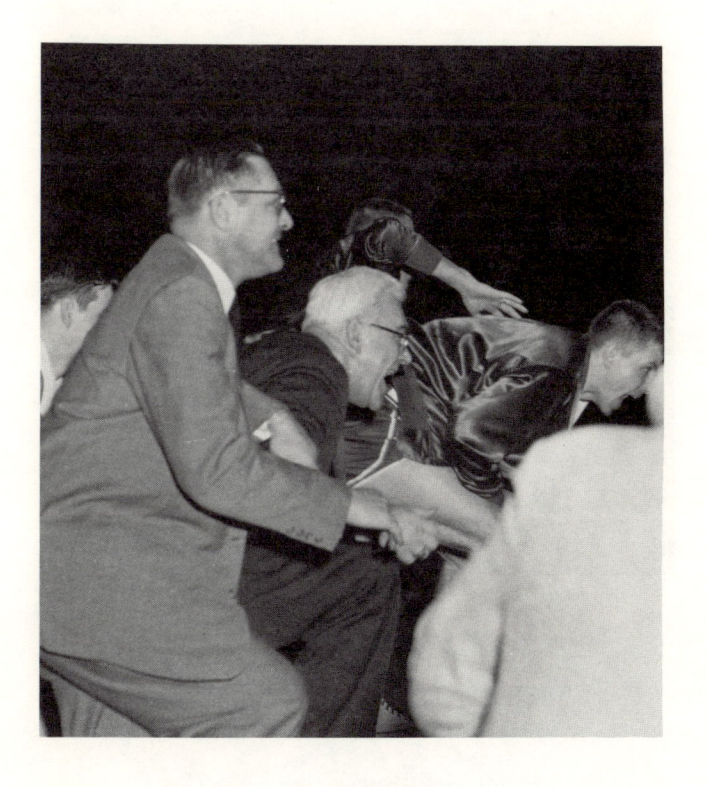

23. Identify this I.U. head coach and assistant coach.

161

Photographs—Questions

24. This is the 1958 NCAA regional locker room. Identify, if you can, the players with Coach McCracken.

162

Photographs—Questions

25. a) Which Van with lay-up?
    b) Who is coming in from his right to follow?

163

Photographs—Questions

26. Can you identify the I.U. coach and three assistants in front of New York's Essex House and decide what they are doing there?

Photographs—Questions

27. Name the tournament, players and reason they are photographed together.

Photographs—Questions

28. Who is the I.U. player on defense?

Photographs—Questions

29. Which I.U. player is injured and what is the occasion?

167

Photographs—Questions

30. Along with Ray Tolbert, which I.U. player is attempting to block this shot?

Photographs—Questions

31. Identify the I.U. player with the lay-up, the player positioned for the rebound and the game.

Photographs—Questions

32. That same great player puts a move on which team on what occasion in which place?

Photographs—Questions

33. Name the occasion, location and I.U. shooter.

Photographs—Questions

34. Woodson watches which I.U. player scramble for the ball?

172

Photographs—Questions

35. Identify the I.U. player ready to pass against Michigan.

Photographs—Questions

36. With Isiah, in the left foreground is which I.U. player? Who is player on the extreme left?

Photographs—Questions

37. What is the place and occasion for I.U.'s celebration? Which I.U. player is in which teammate's arms and who is the I.U. player on the extreme left?

175

Photographs—Questions

38. Who is rebounding for I.U.?

Photographs—Questions

39. Identify the two I.U. players, left to right, and the trophy.

177

Photographs—Questions

40. Who is the I.U. player behind Kent Benson?

Photographs—Questions

41. Who are the I.U. players, one facing us and one with his back to us?

Photographs—Questions

42. Name the trophy and the four I.U. players.

Answers

1. Assembly Hall

2. Memorial Stadium

3. I.U. Fieldhouse on Seventeenth Street

4. The Men's Gymnasium

5. I.U. Fieldhouse on Seventh Street

6. Beck Chapel

7. The Indiana University Memorial Union Building

8. The Well House

Photographs—Answers

9. Showalter Fountain and I.U. Auditorium

10. Jordan

11. The Main Library

12. Dunn Meadow and the Jordan River; east to west

13. Monroe County Courthouse

14. c

15. The Gables

16. The Student Building

17. Maxwell Hall

18. The Student Services Building

19. The Indiana University Memorial Union Building

20. Mike Woodson

21. Tom Abernethy

22. Scott May

23. Branch McCracken in center and assistant coach Ernie Andres on his right

Photographs—Answers

24. From left: front row: Bob Wilkinson, Jerry Thompson, Sam Gee; second row: Archie Dees, Pete Obremsky, Jim Hinds, Bill Balch, Frank Radovich, Allen Schlegelmilch; in back: Ray Ball

25. a) Tom Van Arsdale   b) Tom Bolyard

26. There for the 1985 NIT are Coach Knight and assistants Kohn Smith, behind his right shoulder, Jim Crews, behind his left shoulder, and Royce Waltman, walking toward you near curb with sweater on and hands in pockets.

27. The 1979 NIT; Ray Tolbert on left and Butch Carter were co-MVPs.

28. Jim Crews

29. It is Bobby Wilkerson just after he sustained a concussion in the final NCAA game against Michigan.

30. Landon Turner

31. Isiah Thomas and Steve Risley in the first round of a 1981 NCAA game against Maryland

32. Isiah on UAB in the 1981 regional at Assembly Hall

Photographs—Answers

33. End of first overtime period against Marquette in third game of 1985 NIT at Assembly Hall; Uwe Blab makes a free throw to tie.

34. Kent Benson

35. Steve Green

36. Randy Wittman and Mike LaFave

37. It is Atlanta's Omni in 1984, after I.U.'s victory over North Carolina. Dan Dakich is in Uwe Blab's arms with Courtney Witte on far left.

38. Steve Downing

39. Scott May and Quinn Buckner with the 1976 NCAA championship trophy

40. Jimmy Wisman

41. Butch Carter facing us and Randy Wittman with his back to us

42. The 1981 NCAA championship trophy with, left to right, Glen Grunwald, Steve Risley, Phil Isenbarger and Ray Tolbert